Books by George Bradley

OF THE KNOWLEDGE OF GOOD AND EVIL   *1991*

TERMS TO BE MET   *1986*

Of the Knowledge of Good and Evil

Of the Knowledge

POEMS BY

# of Good and Evil

George Bradley

Alfred A. Knopf   New York   1991

The following poems first appeared in the following publications:

BOULEVARD: "The New Sentimentality"

GRAND STREET: "The Blue Cage," "Chaos, the Theory," *"Deformation Professionnelle,"* *"Noch Einmal, an Orpheus,"* "Objects of Art," "Second Thoughts in Twilight," "Versicles"

THE NEW REPUBLIC: "As the Romans Do," "Keats's Handkerchief," "Notes for an Epigram"

THE NEW YORKER: "Ideal City," *"Nostalgie de la Boue,"* "Of the Knowledge of Good and Evil"

THE PARIS REVIEW: "The 4th of July, and"

PARTISAN REVIEW: "Great Stone Face"

SHENANDOAH: "The Lines Between the Stars," *"La Vie de Bohème,"* "The Year of the Comet"

SOUTHWEST REVIEW: "Lives of the Chinese Poets," "The Panic at Gonesse," "Waiting for Gloria"

VERSE: "Loihi"

WESTERN HUMANITIES REVIEW: "More Perils of Pauline"

THE YALE REVIEW: "Cyclopean Wall in the Alto-Molise"

"Midden" was first printed by Sea Cliff Press as a Christmas greeting.

"Noch Einmal, an Orpheus" was reprinted in *The Best American Poetry, 1988,* published by Charles Scribner's Sons. "Of the Knowledge of Good and Evil," was reprinted in *The Best American Poetry, 1989,* published by Charles Scribner's Sons.

The author thanks the editors of *Southwest Review* for awarding him the Elizabeth Matchett Stover prize for 1989, and the Ingram Merrill Foundation and the National Endowment for the Arts for their assistance.

NOTE: the disagreement mentioned in "Chaos, the Theory" concerns Yale University proper and in no way involves Yale University Press.

Library of Congress Cataloging-in-Publication Data

Bradley, George
    Of the knowledge of good and evil : poems / by George Bradley.
1st ed.
    p.   cm.
    ISBN 0-394-58998-X
    I. Title.
PS3552.R227037   1991   90-53417
811'.54—dc20   CIP

Manufactured in the United States of America
First Edition

Contents

Of the Knowledge of Good and Evil

Sabbath

Upon conversion from their creed
   (The price whereby they might remain),
   It's said what Jews stayed on in Spain
Grew surreptitious out of need,

And when a Friday evening fell,
   They stepped outside among the stars,
   Lit Sabbath candles inside jars
To burn where only God might tell;

So, if they could not lend belief,
   They passed its practice to our day,
   As their descendants just as they
Observe a medieval grief.

Precious, the light that flickers through
   The darkness of an evil time;
   Within the vessel of this rhyme,
Reader, I light a flame for you.

I

Ideal City

Sometimes the weather was nice and time was ample
And you seemed to step forth onto gigantic stones,
To step clear and find yourself in an Ideal City.

It was a place most unlike those grey convolutions,
Those tortuous inclinations, mechanisms of defense,
The medieval warren in which it had been imagined.

Where had been human filth and the communal fosse,
You saw a grand esplanade richly inlaid with marble;
Where were sordid activities and unavoidable violence,

You found doors standing open and not one inhabitant.
How you longed to set out through that city of light,
To stroll under its porticoes, idle among its façades!

But the air you discovered, a blueness run everywhere,
Was the sort of perfection none may breathe, and soon
You and that inhuman order were forced to depart:

You to return to the source of desiring, and it
To struggle up, away, into its own mild sky,
Trying to exist apart, as an idea endowed

With turtledoves and two octagonal wellheads,
With a centrally-planned church and topiary trees,
Like the scene pictured once in the fortified town

Of Urbino and built up in paint years ago
By Bramante, possibly, or by Laurana,
Or by somebody else of like mind.

I'm Sorry, Einstein

*"Newton, forgive me. You found the only way which,
in your age, was just about possible . . ."*

Forgive me, so you said, with what infinite
    Forbearance, with nostalgia, respect,
Apologizing to the past for the thought
    You wreaked, for the order you had wrecked,
For the world itself, the way that it appeared.

Forgive me, you wrote, chagrined, asking pardon
    As if it were your fault for the weird
Way things were, the inexplicability
    Of science, for having persevered
Along a new and difficult dimension

Where time assumes a shape and space bends, where light
    And radiation, not to mention
Matter, may be understood as particles,
    And where the act of apprehension
Is distorted by the place where it occurs,

Or just about possibly so, forgive me.
    Ah Einstein, I'm sorry, but it's worse
Than even you imagined, more beautiful
    And strange, and perhaps the universe
Does not exist except as it is believed,

Or exists only as our motion through it.
    Light, we say, and that's what is perceived;
Nothingness, we think, and find it everywhere.
    I'm sorry, Einstein; oh, I am grieved
To say that perhaps we should apologize

For having learned little, gained so little ground,
    So that each man looks into the skies
And stands where Newton stood, Spinoza, Plato,
    Unsure what he sees with his own eyes,
Discovering an unending darkness flecked
    With the fusion of his own intellect.

A Brief History

Once the world was distant and required imagination,
An anxiety invented out of Abyssinias and Ind, a rumour
Of unusual adornment and a king called Prester John.
Once the horizon hinted, and the sea was a veiled threat.
Heaven was all suspicion then, each mile surmise,
But as all taboo contains its curiosity, in time
The earth surrendered to desire, our importuning,
Sending facts and figures back like Eastern spice,
Yielding its dimensions like so many unknown fruits.
And the world became a succulence, the ripe flesh
Sliding past our palate, the thick juice dripping down,
Fit replacement for the stale confection of ages.
    Morsel of unhedged views, tidbit of flowering plain,
The taste was wholesome and to the tooth, until
An absence was remarked, an omitted piquancy, a tang,
The salt of superstition disappearing from this earth.
Soon clouds were not so strange, soon the dying sun
Did not illuminate its waters as onetime was its wont;
Mapmakers settled down to their projections, and mankind
Awoke the prover of hypotheses, a champion of tomorrow.
    Predictably, uneasy paradise ensued, a shifty-eyed
Evasion of kismet, a studied complacency wherein
Old diseases were wiped out overnight and death became
A lachrymose *faux pas,* the most embarrassing complaint.
But then, even as our final victory was proclaimed,
The earth moved, and it all went wrong in the sky.
When the earth's four corners had been rounded off,
When Chomolungma had been scaled, the oceans plumbed,
When the stars had each been identified and tagged,
And space was subject to high-school science fairs,
Just then, behind the old, a new infinity appeared,
A beaming thing, something energetically waving,
First-class, state-of-the-art, a modern *primum mobile.*
    Fast as the quasar quavers, conclusions fled from us,
While beneath our feet the square inch withdrew,
Retreating before our bold advance with a policy

Of scorched earth and minimal engagement and leaving
A landscape too barren even to be labelled a frontier.
The atoms all but vanished into expressions of a force,
The universe evolved into an impossible description,
And one day it all came clear at last, that moonlight
And the mud, the humblest hearth and siren shores,
Were scenery, of course, but in the theatrical sense,
Effects achieved as always with mirrors and with smoke.

   And in that new epiphany our fear came flooding back,
All our instinct for unknowing, our capacity for doubt;
Trepidation was restored, and we welcomed its misgiving,
Embracing an emotion that had trickled from our hearts;
We hoisted high the burden we had once been used to bear
And laughed to feel its weight, wept at its return,
Eager in the exercise of what we knew best how to do
And rejoicing in confusion, in the abject awe
That chafed and was our true talent, and so remained.

Cyclopean Wall in the Alto-Molise

Having come far, across mountains and the sea,
Over the landscape of fierce superstition
And off the ocean of forgotten years,
They reached a site of upland meadows stark
Against the sky, of stones and stony streams,
A region dark with clouds and shade of trees.
What they arrived at they pronounced as theirs,
The harsh climate, the difficult terrain,
Possessed it in the name of patrimony,
Of refuge and retreat, the name of home;
They claimed that earth and set themselves to labor,
To build the necessary difference,
The wall that separated what they thought
Themselves to be from all they could imagine.
High ground, a few huts, a pool of water:
What they secluded wasn't of importance,
Just that there be some barrier between
The world they made and the great world beyond,
The hills that wandered off, the stars that stayed,
And so they heaved the boulders into place,
Cut the cunning joints and made them balance,
Constructing something where it hadn't been.
It worked, or seemed to, for awhile, for years
In which they lived as they expected, died
As they were told, in which their prayers called forth
Responses and their rituals were observed.
That huge wall hides nothing now, nor grave
Nor habitation, custom nor nostalgia,
So that its blocks are once more of a piece
With land that sweeps from La Maiella's peak
Down toward Campobasso in the south;
Today the wall keeps nothing in or out,
Because the world outside returned (although
The crops grew and opponents grew no stronger),

Because the outside world always returns,
Creeping over rows of fallen dreams
To smudge distinctions and erase each line,
The world, the infinite surround.

Lives of the Chinese Poets

About suffering they were reticent,
Their own at any rate, preferring delicate descriptions
Of fruit trees in bloom to the tale of lives spent
In loneliness, exile, poverty,
Their own portion of the unbearable conditions
Endemic to a civilization continually in collapse.
Intrigue might poison a career, friends be banished, ministers be
     strangled in their beds;
Perhaps famine would afflict the Empire, uprisings start, or perhaps
Horsemen would pour in from the north, plowing the Emperor's
     city
Into pasture land and piling the heads of children into hideous
     pyramids;
Public catastrophe, private ruin, awaited each turn of events,
But the Chinese poets
Observed how starlight leapt among the fishing boats,
How sunlight sent shadows creeping along a garden fence.

Consider the case of Yüan Chen, who was styled
A genius by his contemporaries and died in the year 831.
Subtle of thought, unsubtle of speech, Yüan was frequently exiled,
To Hupeh, to Kwangsi, to Szechwan,
Absences that cost his wife and child their lives.
One evening, in a remote village and among uneducated men,
He looked past the curtain fluttering in the casement
At the world outside his cottage and made this assessment:
The blossoms fall quietly, one by one, wrote Yüan Chen,
But no one else arrives.

Notes for an Epigram

Heraclitus, whose work comes down to us in tatters,
Mere fragments preserved in the works of other authors,
Is said to have believed that there is no truth
But yields, sufficiently considered, to broader definition;
And thus the entire history of Western Thought,
That elaborate edifice assembled brick by brick,
That symmetrical and heavily-fortified construct
Founded finally on air, might be said to be
A refutation of the empirical relativism of Heraclitus,
Though today's Analytical Philosophy says something very like.
O most fortunate Heraclitus! Of whose wisdom
The pearls alone are remembered, and who now,
After some reflection, even appears to be right.

Keats's Handkerchief

One day you, also, will gaze into Keats's handkerchief
And find, with him, the evidence, ghastly, glistening,
Of your mortality, the crimson drop of arterial blood
Your tubercular cough has deposited in that cloth.
Someday an immense future will simply disappear.
When that day comes, don't think yourself surprised,
Though you seem young, though your ambition, Caesarean,
Alexandrine, has been left grotesquely unfulfilled—
All men are young, everything remains to do, and hope
Is a companion that should always have died hereafter.
And don't pretend ignorance, spare yourself such deceit,
Though cold and adamantine fingers grip your heart
And your breath labor with the weight of what you know—
Having been studious, having made your soul in the vale
Of human possibilities, it is this you have prepared for:
To recognize and record your perception and its passing.
Stare in that woven square and consider the thing at hand.
If you could sever yourself from its fell significance
It might seem even beautiful, the gleaming bead of blood
As rare as gemstone, a ruby of the finest water,
Bright as Betelgeuse in the glittering cloth of night.
Stare awhile, and then put the handkerchief away;
Take up your brother's hand, who lies in pain,
For poor Tom is dying, too.

The Blue Cage

The universe composed itself around a door,
Now that the happy sun and its attendant clouds
Had drifted off in valedictory display.
Walls rose up where open fields had stretched,
And stars pressed down their thin white light;
Beneath his feet, all dead things heaved.
His universe was distance and this door,
Stone gate, grated portal, shuttered aperture,
Great pillars standing at earth's end.
It was the door that made the sky so blue,
The door that gave each instant its tiny tick.
Within were robust wines, garlic and legumes,
Was water, certainly, catching the last bright rays;
Without, dust in the mouth, a sustenance of wind.
All space was blue bars and this one door,
And he hovered at the threshold, kneeling there
As angels do, to speak the prescribed syllables.
Oh, it was not the habitation he had expected,
The huge expanse that beckoned, unpeopled place,
That other ocean, bodiless and lapping.
But the mind never finds the way it will not pass:
He stood up and walked out of this world.

Noch Einmal, an Orpheus

When the Queen of Darkness heard his voice,
That mortal stranger, saw him lift the lyre
And watched the dull throng of the dead rejoice
To hear him tell of earth and earth's desire,
Of pain, of longing, she was not amused.
She caught that veiled allusion to the shame
Of her own story and would have refused
Him then and there, had not the shades that came
In droves now clamoured so for his request.
"Be rid of him," she breathed to the immense
Stillness at her side, who thought it best
To play a cruel joke at the man's expense,
Fated as he was to indecision,
To second thoughts, a lifetime of revision.

Waiting for Gloria

for my mother and father

The hurricane of 1938
Happened on this shoreline by surprise,
As what had been a tropical depression
Of only average size
While forming on the Caribbean seas
Expanded with the moisture-laden breeze
Of Florida to grow depressed indeed,
A barometric nightmare gaining speed
Off Hatteras and shifting in its course
By dark, so that it outran all alarms
And fell with unanticipated force
Upon Long Island's cottages and farms,
Leaving less occasion to prepare
Than if the crack of doom had sounded there.
   It almost did, from what old-timers say:
Propelled a hundred forty miles per hour,
Thin air assumes an awe-inspiring power,
And anything that cannot crouch must fly;
Whatever will not weather must give way
When record rainfall tumbles from the sky
To climb above ten inches in one day.
Arriving at high tide,
The storm plowed salt into the countryside,
And crops till then protected from the brine
Were blasted by the spray;
So, in the blink of that cyclonic eye,
The seasons altered in an afternoon,
The fruits of autumn wasting on the vine
Without a hint of frost or harvest moon.
As if by some design,
The hurricane struck hardest at the spot
Where houses flourished and the dunes did not:
The ocean leapt across Westhampton Beach
To raze the shingle summer homes it found,
While residents, left clinging each to each,
Were swept away and for the most part drowned,

18

Their cries submerged in the unheard of sound
Of wind that whistled by at such a rate
That everything it touched must resonate.
  Within two hours the storm passed overhead,
Bound for New London, Providence, New Hampshire,
And left Long Island sorting out its dead;
It was the sort of murderous event
You read about in the Old Testament,
A wind to shake the earth, and in its wake
Lay ruin unrelieved, as the entire
New England coast was battered at the cost
Of more destruction and of more life lost
Than that reported in Chicago's fire
Or San Francisco's quake.
That hurricane killed seven hundred people
And washed away the Montauk fishing fleet.
It toppled maple and uprooted birch—
Three hundred million trees—and felled the steeple
Beside the old Sag Harbor whalers' church
That faces Union Street.
It put the putrid odor in the air
Of rotting livestock scattered everywhere
And plucked a hatchway from my family's roof
So that the rain-soaked ceilings sagged and fell,
A *coup de grâce* to end the Great Depression.
In thirty-eight, a world was blown to hell
By weather worse than folks had ever had,
And now they say what's coming is as bad.
  "You'd think the human race might learn a lesson,"
My father, standing on a ladder, mutters
At a vista which, from this height, seems
A quilt of tennis courts and swimming pools
Pulled snug around some architect's bad dreams,
"Still building on the beach, the ruddy fools."
My answer is to hand him down the shutters
We're taking from the dormer window frames
To keep the wind from dashing them to bits
In less than no time when the first squall hits;
Time was, he could have done it on his own,
But one old man can't keep a country home
In times like these, and therefore I have come,

Drawn from the city by the storm report,
To cart off any trash that might be blown
About and lash the woodpile down, to nail
The barn doors fast and tape the window glass,
To locate lamps and fill the cars with gas
And, foreseeing that the pump will fail,
To run some extra water in the bath,
To lay in food and candles and, in short,
To do what can be done in last resort
When trouble's up and you are in its path.
    In this case trouble has a name, although
Such things didn't fifty years ago:
Gloria, which we think a happy choice,
Instead of something plain or just plain odd,
For what is billed to be a cross between
A freak of nature and the hand of God.
The news puts Gloria just an hour offshore,
And now the ocean's melancholy voice
Is building to a roar,
While small rain driven by the rising gale
Already stings my skin; as thick clouds sail
Through a lowering sky, like landscape seen
In passing from a train, the morning light
Of mid-September turns a shade of green;
Leaves and twigs and blades of grass take wing,
All wildlife vanishes, and no birds sing.
    I take a final shutter from its hooks
And pause, our task complete, to gaze around
Before we go. I'd say my father's right:
Built with slight support on sandy ground,
Those million dollar mansions on the dunes
Seem all but outward bound.
"They'll go like *that*," the old man likes to say,
"Clean out to sea," and from the way it looks,
Today might be the day
In which the clutter grown up with the years
On what had been the countryside of youth
(Houses strewn where he can still see fields,
New-made roads with names that do not mean
A thing to him, who now can best retain
The world that was when he was seventeen)

Wobbles and with one puff disappears,
Dispersed, as much as by the hurricane,
By wishful thinking realized at last,
Just as the present, stormed by memory, yields
To better judgment and becomes the past.

   "Five letters, anyone, for 'mend mistakes'?"
My mother, puzzled by the *Times,* inquires
Of us the instant we are back inside.
Before the fireplace, where she's set her chair,
With pun and pencil at her tongue, she shakes
Her head and smiles when Father offers 'blast,'
Then frowns and writes as I suggest 'erase.'
Given cunning words and cozy fires,
Mother takes her hurricanes in stride
And laughs to hear me say it's all hot air.
"Anything to eat around this place?"
Puts my father, perfectly content
To see the wind and water do their worst
So long as he has filled his belly first;
And Mother, even as His Hunger speaks,
Has much to recommend,
For knowing that this meal might be the end
Of comfort for some days or even weeks,
She's occupied the hours the menfolk spent
Aloft providing for their wants below,
Gathering a luncheon that will go
From soup to nuts to flutes of Veuve Cliquot:
A choice repast, assembled with such art
It seems like sacrilege to lift a fork.

   A phone pole staggers as I pop the cork—
It only takes our sitting down to eat
To make the world around us fall apart—
Trees sag and split amidst a cloud of leaves,
While power lines lie writhing in the street,
So that just as I propose a toast,
Our electricity gives up the ghost;
Above the beach, a pounding ocean heaves
Up bursts of spray to blossom in the sky
Like fireworks that explode there in July;
We watch a neighbor's home as shingles lift
Off one by one, while underneath our door

The rain leaks in and pools up on the floor.
The rafters creak, the boards begin to shift,
The whole house shudders like a ship at sea,
And even Mother starts to show the strain;
But Father, his disgust replacing glee,
Just stares and grumbles, "not enough debris."
   As shredded vegetation coats each pane
Of glass, the spectacle becomes obscure,
A scene of clouded rage and dim excess;
It looks as if the landscape can't endure
The site of so much self-destructiveness,
But when we think the world won't stand the pace,
The wind drops and the sun reveals its face,
House lights for a hasty intermission
Of fifteen minutes while we're in the eye.
A heavy calm prevails, and then the sky
Boils over once again, the remnant scenery
Reverting to a supplicant position,
Bent beneath the will of winds reversed,
Which force the loosened trunks of listing greenery
To stand straight up and fall the other way.
Yet this act seems less violent than the first,
And knowing how a drama, once begun,
Becomes a bore if it is overdone,
We wonder if we've grown a bit blasé,
Till someone's not-too-educated guess
Surmises now the storm is in recess,
Its forward motion sped to the other shores,
The wind that circles back to us is less.
It's still enough to make the chimney scream
And rattle glass and crack a basement beam,
And then it's over, and we step outdoors.
   Surveying the effects from our front lawn,
We might be dreamers waking from the dream,
Amazed to see the sun
Return us all we'd thought to leave behind.
"I hope those weathermen were having fun,"
My father says. "There's not a damned thing gone."
And sure enough, a spindrift gaze will find
That not one beach-house has been undermined;
But if such human elements remain,

With every rooted thing the race is run:
Mother's flower garden lies in tatters,
And this year's bloom is blown. It hardly matters,
Though, for standing in the gentle breeze
That's been imported freshly from the Keys,
You'd say that any loss had been our gain;
You'd say the sky had never been so clear,
The way the storm has scrubbed the atmosphere,
And swear the air had never smelled so good,
Now that the winnowed grass and broken wood
Send up their scent like heavenly refrains,
Like incense, like the desert when it rains,
What perfume would resemble if it could.
  Have you ever seen this earth the day
A hurricane blows by? You feel a great
Peace descend, and life seems sweet, the way
It must have seemed that time in thirty-eight,
In spite of all destruction and decay.
Those passed-over best appreciate
What world we have, who know each overcast
Will clear in time, and know this calm can't last.

II

Midden

Under the siftings, strata, the great upheavals,
Beneath the flowing, breaking, the many folds,
When he came upon them, objects of curiosity,

It was their shards and discards he knew them by,
The superstitious, the pained, the cunning ones,
Who had wheedled daybreak and bullied twilight

Until the blue diurnal domes became with time
A sort of home to the paltry things they were
And to what they suffered, the ideas they had,

Until the residuum of the simplest life they led
Gained in substance, acquired the quiet dignity,
Becoming a declaration of days under that sun,

Evidence of their expressions, of words they spoke,
Until the bits of clay, the pointed sticks, became
A legacy, their accumulation and accomplishment.

The Uncertainty Principle

The world is what it seems, be it bubble or the bell
That rings to rouse the paralegal and timely tolls
Him back to sleep; the world is flat or round, a hoop
To knot contortionists and make the small dog leap,
Or pointed as to spur ascetics into shades of weight
They were, gastric nonconformists in alimentary flight
From maya, from illusion, the unfaithful fetching face.
A ripple of astonishment and strange substantial rays,
The world is as it seems, and that it seems the catch
(That surface is all likelihood, perception just a hunch)
Compels the scientist to postulate a view so circumspect.
It seems the world comes compromised in waves that interact,
Comes as a shadow cast by something standing in a sun,
And since the nature of the energy entailed in observation
Instils its own disturbance, its tiny flutter of retort,
Within that decadent display—oh, here's the beauty part—
Beneath these beams we can't make out the loci of the motes,
Must make our guess instead, the subatomic stab that sets
Us free to see waves as particles, if this should satisfy,
See particles as waves, if it simplify equation, free.
Well, there you have it then, a world still unexplained,
A question begged, the idiotic answer to an anserine demand;
The world is its arcanum still, and its precept to perplex,
Uncertainty as Principle become the fundament of physics,
Which (having had an Age of Reason and centuries of progress,
Given our taste for revelation and our abiding animus
Against any ambiguity that comes unescorted by an angel)
Is the sort of oxymoron that might almost make you smile,
The way you'd smile to give your mathematics teacher
The news that nowadays, what with pocket calculators,
Computerized you-name-it, and accountants for everyone,
You don't need introductory algebra to reach the moon,
Much less grow up and be a president or poet . . .
But the victory is small (10^{-9} cm at most), to gloat
Is unattractive, and heaven knows your math tutor did try.
Besides, the thing at issue has never been Uncertainty,

Not ever the undecided, but rather the strict reverse,
This requisite, at once risible and grave, our exercise
Of carrying a nothingness to put it nowhere down,
Shifting unseen weight over an ever-shifting terrain
And under the undulant air, and putting in our comments
Vis-à-vis particulars, the while we travel, owls to Athens.

Chaos, the Theory

As nothing is isolated of an agency, no sweeping and no speck,
As no man or woman, flake or flash, is insulated of effect,
And as the whole precarious thing extant is poised each instant
On the precipitous verge of random cause and rational result,
Who is to say the gigantic sun that leaps up this day,
Or a blade of grass that bends beneath my feet,
Or a cricket that sings in China,
Or the $700 Yale University
Agreed to pay me and did not,
Might not ultimately be the spur that sends this world, this
    universe,
Over a cataract whose presence and proportions we but dimly
    conceive
Into an unforeseeable but familiar pattern of catastrophe?
What is to say this poem won't tip the scales toward cosmic
    disaster?
We the believers, the converts, fervid evangels,
Know no deliberation or dim idea that goes lost or unremarked.
Though we gaze on swirling waters, though the future be ever
    closed,
Though an order so delicately responsive must seem disorder
    always,
Yet nothing comes to pass without incalculable event.
Our creed is chaos, its sudden starts and jagged edge:
We asseverate each thought is of unimagined potency,
We appoint each grain of sand the fulcrum of an age.

The Panic at Gonesse

In the year 1783
   when Paris was the center
    of a western world
that still revolved around royalty,
   when revolution was in
    the air, though the old
order was the order of the day,
   when science had recently
    come into fashion,
though wearing wigs was not yet passé,
   when Ben Franklin was special
    envoy to Versailles,
mankind first discovered how to fly.
   Rumour reached the capital
    of a smoke-filled bag
rising fifteen hundred feet above
   a village outside Lyons,
    and a Monsieur Charles,
part physicist and part mountebank
   (said in some salons to be
    illegitimate
son to a marquis), realized he
   could realize a profit
    on modernity.
He floated subscriptions to the sight
   of a similar display,
    while commissioning
the construction of a twelve foot sphere,
   to be made of taffeta
    that had been infused
with rubber dissolved in turpentine;
   this testament to progress
    processed by torchlight
through the city streets in the small hours
   of August twenty-seventh
    to the Champs de Mars,

there to be inflated with a gas
    produced by a thousand pounds
        of iron filings
subjected to sulphuric acid.
    The result was the world's first
        hydrogen balloon,
which by some miracle of science
    behaved not as it ought to,
        but as expected,
swelling and straining at the guy-ropes
    rather than of an instant
        consuming the crowd
in the vivid spectacle of flames.
    As the balloon filled with gas,
        so the sky with clouds,
dampening the enthusiasm
    of the assembled voyeurs
        with a fitful rain.
Preparations dragged on through the day,
    as a crude experiment
        using navigant
triangulation was ironed out,
    whereby watches and quadrants
        at three vantage points
were to pinpoint the sphere in the sky;
    a pennant run up a pole
        and a cannon blast
were to synchronize the instruments
    and to accompany the launch,
        but as the weather
worsened and those gathered grew restive
    and five hundred pounds of hot
        sulphuric acid
threatened, with the admixture of rain,
    to send up the scientists
        and science alike,
the craft was released ahead of time
    to rise without benefit
        of report or flag
and disappear inside two minutes
    into the low cloud cover,

into history,
into the collective memory
and the artists' renderings.
As the crowd dispersed,
the sphere sailed unobserved to a field
some fifteen miles away, where
it fell from the sky
among peasants gathering their grain,
for whom events at Paris
were a distant dream,
for whom clouds normally held no more
than the unwelcome prospect
of a spoiled harvest;
they fell upon the thing, piercing it,
beating it, dragging it to
the nearby village
of Gonesse, not far from what is now
the airport of Le Bourget,
outside Ecouen.
There the contemporary etchings
surprise them, with the balloon
hitched behind a horse,
a suspicious circle of rustics
armed with sickles, flails and forks,
captured in the act
of becoming a footnote to flight,
as well as the laughingstock
of all of Paris,
where the scene was the rage that season
among lords and ladies of
the *ancien régime*,
who could not know what panic the march
of progress might hold in store
for them, what terror
(say one afternoon amidst a crowd
in the Place de la Concorde)
drop from overhead.

Objects of Art

In his elegant hand the jeweler might
Fill prescriptions fit for an ailing queen—
Obsidian, moss agate, rhodonite,
Lapis-lazuli, chased gold, tourmaline,
Opals, emeralds, nephrite, purpurine—
So spring resurfaces in *guilloché,*
A sentiment expressed in swag and screen,
As the Empress accepts each Easter day
An opulent egg from the firm of Fabergé.

Jasper, jade, chalcedony, cabochon
Cut rubies, silver niello, peridot—
Karl Gustavovich and *frère* Agathon
Cater to customers whose taste for show
Was not quite exhausted by rococo;
Baffling craft and iridescent palettes
Become a style of art, the *art nouveau,*
In which dispassionate firing begets
The alloyed pleasure of a case for cigarettes,

Or cards, or powder, or any object
Of lapidary fantasy to which
The most jaded fancy could not object.
Patterns from the past, stones out of a ditch,
The world and time for Karl Gustavovich
Exist to be perfected in a thing
Of beauty made for placement in a niche,
An idea finished in enamelling,
A swan so fine it takes the eye as taking wing.

1914, and Alexandra's gift
Is platinum, with square-cut gems and bands
Of pearls; if pressed, a hidden lid will lift
To yield a mounted cameo that stands
Adorned with diamonds, with floral garlands,
And with her children—what an egg contains,
What the heart desires and the age demands—
The precious thoughts an Empress entertains
As snow falls in the courtyard and confusion reigns.

More Perils of Pauline

So this is what it comes down to, fruit of the fabulous
Tales, those knights in shining stories dwindled
To this, a hectoring of the emotions,
A farce by flickering light.
Skittish ingenue coiled in crude turns of plot,
Pauline is no less than this century deserves,
Culture finding its own level even as water will;
Yet if our heroine protest too much to high heaven,
Still who can fail to be affected or ignore
The sudden stab that attends our recognition—
Behind that halo of hair, the hand held to the mouth—
Of Iseult borne over waters to misfortune,
Angelica madding through the groves,
Helen waiting for the menfolk to start up?
Sad in its way, like a lover met after long absence,
And hence the vague melancholy sure to stain
Our pleasure, even as we cheer and stomp our feet,
The sheepishness that escorts us from the theater.
Mixed feelings, to be sure, but they will have to do,
Because such show is what we have, and the feelings
Want to be there. Besides, Pauline's story is really our own,
Our way of living from crisis to unlikely crisis,
The absurd fixes we will get into,
The terror that defines us,
And who can resist screaming when we hear
The buzz-saw whine, the locomotive whistle its approach,
Grasping that our torment and our rescue
Will be one and the same and in the nick of time?

Deformation Professionnelle

How nice to think it was a thing that care
Could have avoided, a fate Mama warned of
And was right after all, a misery traceable
To wet mittens, to drafts and bad company.
How pleasant to wish it might be no cause
For despair, might be an excidable thing,
An odd but operable growth on one's *bonhomie*.
But you knew the blythe spirit necessary
To sustain such fleet fantastic flights
Begged an almost physical performance,
Demanded the sort of mental gymnastic
Peculiar to the lovely ignorance of youth,
Knew, after so many hours of repetition,
After careful imitation, studied response,
That your convictions, your poisonous disbelief,
Your disembodied shame before each sun,
Were a truck driver's bad back, a cowboy's
Gimpy gait, a ballerina's tender, twisted feet.
Shhh. Music is playing. The darkness explodes.
A figure hangs its gorgeous instant in space,
Leaning into the light, before the delicate,
Tentative toe descends again to a blaze
Of shooting pain and bloody bandages;
And we also descend, out of the unlimited,
Alien air, to the observable friction
And scarcely concealed sorrow of our lives.

La Vie de Bohème

A friend of friends, a sojourner
Among exiles, he survived it seemed
On sufferance, someone-or-thing's,
A hanger-on about places haunted
By expatriates; the world he lived in,
The café, the pension, the boulevard,
Seemed never quite his own, seemed
Unnecessary, was never home to one
Who inhabited so many worlds at once;
And yet the Mercurey fell in the glass
For him as well, and frost bloomed
On his window like a giant's breath.
For him also the cold came, for him
Wind rose and all rains fell.

To put no faith in any world but suffer
This one still, that was his misery,
The grief he came to first, before
He had a name for grievance
Or syllables for such a thought.
Hence leather pants and anisette,
Hence pink gloves and postures;
But pastiche nor *pastis* could please him,
For whom the gypsy songs were stale,
For whom Mimi and the brightest hearth
Held no more warmth than starlight,
And here was a corollary complaint,
To suffer this world just the same
But to get none of its good.
So in the house of happiness
He became an advocate, a subvert,
A disbeliever among that flock.

Into many a little lamb's tipsy ear
He whispered his grim *pensées,*
And the wry smile of mockery
Writhed always upon his lips;
And yet his evil intimations
Brought forth but blythe reply,
Brought forth the fond response
That was to be his final woe,
That grotesque words should satisfy
No more than sweet, the earth spin
Will-he-nill-he, insincere sphere.
To be so at the edge of things, to be
Extraneous, became his last despair,
And so reduced he grew a creature,
An element, an equanimity, an X,
For whom sunshine could fall as snow,
For whom bitterness and joy lay bleached
As bones upon a beach, lay leeched
Of any dread, lay as objects on a table,
A *crème glacée,* a *café avec du zest.*

So it was he lived his life at last
As theory, as a grand hypothesis,
Propounding elegant phrases on the *rive,*
Observing formalities in the park;
And when the dust blown in the square
Inquired also after him, he imagined
An orchestral movement, a symphony,
Trumpets, cymbals, *vivace con moto,*
He thought of velvet robes, why not,
He beheld a golden chariot in air,
He saw splendors of *son et lumière,*
Oh why not have it that way,
In the light that fell on him as he lay,
In that thin, that inaccessible day.

The New Sentimentality

It is just possible, of course, that this fascination
With nothingness is only one more histrionic mood,
A sentimental overlay like moonlight on the shore,
Is impression, emotion, a music put upon the place.
It might be that our preoccupation, morbid and perverse,
With an empty universe is but a satisfaction of the mind,
An illusion sweetly held as our inmost sugared thought,
That the coldnesses we cultivate like arctic ice
Heaped up in wild blue blocks against the polar sky
Might be mint chocolates, cheap scent, a genre scene,
A Christmastime of the incorrigible imagination.
The mind sees nothing long and too long, and perhaps
The wind that gallops across the glacier, whipping
White flurries before it like clouds blown overhead,
Is no more dignified or true than our tenderest conceit.
The restless waters, the locked earth, the far stars
Are things our thoughts will cling to while they can,
But perhaps we ought to look beyond the oscillations
Of belief that flicker in our brains like candlelight,
Like all the energy there is blinking on and off,
Pulsating, sputtering, soaring though billions of years,
To whatever exists untouched by the distortion of ideas.
The light keeps rushing down and everything it meets—
Oceans of time, the dustmites in the mattress, ourselves—
Responds, joins hands to dance in blissful circles.
Go on then, get the mail, make friends, pat the dog.
In every ray that passes, our paradise is taking place.

Fool, Said My Muse to Me,

Look in, for the purely mechanical
Function may be more telling than ideals
You think to hold at heart, than all manner
Of constructed sound, our rag-tag efforts
To commiserate, more even than thought
Itself, searching out its dissolutions,
So that the dumb persistent little fist
May seem, beat by beat, all that we will be.
Exquisite in its way, as it absorbs
The influx of its surroundings, it leaps
At each occasion to extrude the same,
And yes, it is what we can know of love,
Convulsed, compulsive, our life-long support
And soon enough our complete undoing.

The 4th of July, and

The sidewalks are wobbling in the god-awful heat,
　　Ninety-eight in the shade,
Where there is shade, as New York lies locked under
　　Layers of high pressure
That trap the thick atmosphere (ozone, exhaust, smog
　　Drifted over from Jersey,
Infernal dampness: "It's not the heat, it's the whatchamacallit,"
　　Said a fat girl in the elevator,
Too hot or too humid to get a grip on her clichés),
　　Clapping it over your face:
Today, Independence Day, on the verge of moving to the burbs
　　(7 rms, 2 bths, occ. negotiable),
I walk to the window (how the black dust seeps in!) and look
　　Upon the city I am losing:
Lines for everything, jack-hammers, crime, garbage,
　　Rent out the wazoo,
Air pollution, noise pollution, rush-hour traffic, dope,
　　Payola, beautiful people,
Bag people, a new disease every day, cyclical poverty,
　　Mayor Koch (yech),
Donald Trump (yech, yech), Leona Helmsley (STOP!):
　　Why even Sandy McClatchy,
Who, let's face it, is a man at pains to appear urbane,
　　When he got back last time
Said this town seems more and more like Calcutta,
　　So why, can you tell me,
After ten years of such dreck should I be sorry to go?
　　I mean, should I care?
Because, excuse me, fresh bagels all by themselves
　　Can't make up for it all,
Not even from H & H World's Best Bagels, where the sign says
　　"You'll be in Heaven—Share Them!!!"
(O.K.: oh to be standing in the March a.m. with a hot bagel
　　In your hand, its soft flesh
Yielding to your fingers and the steam rising into your face . . .
　　Mmmm, make mine with raisins).

But today, Independence Day, as a huge, hazy, orange sun
   Sets over the Bayonne swamps
Like an industrial disaster, like gas flaring over an oil field,
   Why give a second thought,
Can you tell me please, to the notion of kissing goodbye
   Cabbies who know everything
And got off the boat just last week? of leaving behind
   Cops with that big-city attitude
And that high school education? of bidding a final *adieu*
   To the Eurotrash crowding midtown?
Why is the heart downcast to think I won't be seeing
   The promenade along the Heights
(Alright, I don't go there all that often, but I *could*),
   Where I chatted with Ben Gardner
The third time he got off the ward? We availed ourselves
   Of that view and spoke of how,
Statistically considered, the odds were his mind would now
   Never really be right again.
And what of the old-world roses in back of the Brooklyn Museum?
   If you time your visit right
(The 4th of July is too late, early June would be better),
   You can take in Albert Bierstadt
And then find Coral Creeper in bloom, pale apricot and smelling
   Sweeter even than oil paint.
Or if that seems too out-of-town (those Japanese tour groups
   Just *love* botanical gardens),
We speeding bedlamites might cross the bridge and drop
   By Chumley's for a drink:
Left over from prohibition, Chumley's is all a bar should be,
   Dark and cool, even in July,
And decorated with book jackets by authors famous in their time.
   Let's have gin gimlets
(Just gin and lime juice, no additives—New York bartenders
   Will try to be original)
And look around the place, at the wood paneling and stone hearth
   And two inconspicuous exits,
Still a handy feature if you see someone you'd rather not.
   Now that we've started
Who wants to stop? Let's do them all, let's hit the White Horse
   Where Hudson St. winds up

(Only, please, this once, could we get in and out without quoting
     His Welsh and blottoed self?);
Let's taxi along Park Ave. to the lounge at the Mayfair Regent
     And sit in wing-back chairs
While the girls in victorian garb bring us exotic rum punches;
     Let's take the tube to Tribeca,
To Puffy's on Varick St. (yes, I know Puffy's is all yuppies now—
     Too close to the exchanges,
And besides, artists can't afford Tribeca anymore—but today
     Everyone's left for the 4th
And we can drink in peace as the trucks coming out of the tunnel
     Rumble past warehouses outside).
Look, let's really celebrate—come on, I'm leaving this town—
     I know an opium den
Not far from the Manhattan Bridge (that engineering embarrassment,
     That rickety hodgepodge,
That architectural macaronic of gothic arches and filigree finials
     And some sort of Brandenburg Gate
Providing triumphal entry to the stoplights along Flatbush Ave.),
     And if we beg at the door
We might just get in, even though we don't speak Chinese
     And have big noses and smell bad.
What do you mean you don't want to? What else is New York for?
     Costly hangovers and a cheap ennui,
So come on, and since we're half-drunk and headed that direction,
     Let's stop at Diamond Lil's,
The joint on Canal where Rick Tilton used to get flat polluted
     As he drank and drew the dancers
(All the models a painter could ask for, right there on the bar,
     And striking *most* unusual poses),
Only—damn!—I forgot, Diamond Lil's became McDonald's, and that
     Is the trouble with this town:
Just when you get used to it, get to know your way around,
     The city you have learned is gone,
Torn down and made over according to someone else's blueprint
     Of how New York should be,
The landscape of your desires replaced by one more up-to-date,
     By something more profitable
(Building New York making politicians so much money they elect
     To repeat the effect regularly),

So that if you go looking for McFeely's, in the Terminal Hotel
    At the west end of 23rd,
Where Dan Halpern and Stephen Spender came in to eat one night
    With a copy of Schuyler's poem
Called "Dining Out with Doug and Frank," which takes place there,
    And started reading it aloud
Without even noticing—dumb bunnies—that sitting right next to them
    Were Doug and Frank in the flesh,
You'll find it's closed, kaput, in renovation, i.e. done for;
    And if you go looking
At the head of Macdougal for the Eighth St. Bookstore,
    Where my poems will never stand
Between Byron and Blake (and right next to Charles Bukowski:
    Sometimes life is pure bathos),
You'll find it's disappeared, vanished like volumes out-of-print,
    Literally gone up in smoke,
And if New York has its bookstores still, still none of them,
    Not Gotham Bookmart
(It's clubby and confuses literature with rock n' roll, but stocks
    Plenty of poetry anyway),
Not Books & Co. (spruce, with a so-so poetry selection unaccountably
    Interspersed with prose),
Not the Phoenix, Gryphon, St. Marks, not Coliseum, not the Strand,
    No none of them approach
That paragon, that platonic ideal, that paradise of bibliophiles,
    Eighth St. Bookstore of my mind!
And that, of course, is the landfill it's all been dragged to,
    The suburb it's all moved into,
The city of my recollection become the province of idle thought,
    Its buildings suddenly transported,
Transformed into an imagined land, a half-visible locale
    Where Kim Rogal and David Kalstone
(Each genial, myopic, bemused) may still be found at parties;
    Where some celluloid *obscurité*
Still shows nightly to the faithful lined up outside the Thalia
    (Inside are popcorn-eating mice
And the feeling of being between decks on a tramp steamer);
    Where those old synagogues
On the lower east side, with their snakey, oriental motifs,
    And those upper west side churches,

With their quasi-military towers and turrets, all still stand
    (Churches are like women for me . . .
Worship seems a bit excessive, but I do like to look at them),
    And the trashy condos
That replaced them are stripped, gutted, dynamited, razed;
    Where the Day Line still plies
Hudson's River, pushing upstream all the way to Poughkeepsie
    To return among green prospects
Past Storm King and the Tappan Zee, past the Palisades
    (That beetling escarpment
In which geologic time is evident as writing on the wall),
    Back to New York, Sin City,
Wick to the wicked and home to eight million aspirations:
    City of unnatural light,
City of squalor and big ambition, O infinitely human city,
    Your every aspect I have
At heart from this day Fourth as the secret that defines me,
    A Central Park of the soul,
Composed of all the beauty and violence that is the past,
    A darkening confine from which
Patens of memory will rise like poems, like the explosions
    That have now begun to burst
Above the Park, above the Battery (when I lived in Brooklyn,
    In a factory in the ghetto,
Holidays would bring fireworks over Manhattan and brisk reports
    Of gunfire throughout Fort Green),
In radiant showers of red and white and blue, a first-class farewell,
    A really super send-off,
The simply dazzling evanescence ("one lollapalooza of a show!"
    "Rip-snorting entertainment!"
"Mesmerizing, jaw-gritting excitement!") that is what I take away
    On July 4th 1988, Independence Day.

III

Second Thoughts in Twilight

He kept coming back to this impoverished world,
To its tattered beauty, sudden transformations,
Kept returning, though he knew what he would find,

Though the dazed people would be plodding along,
Though the place could hold no more surprises, still
He would come back, as to a lover, to a thought.

He knew the sky could not amaze him as before,
Yet he returned to see it all take place again,
To see the nimbused clouds and shafts of light,

To watch the islands sink into the western sea
And observe the shy appearance of the crescent moon
As it put off its veil of sunshine and stepped forth.

He came to see the darkened fields, mown meadows,
To witness falling stars that spent themselves in space
Like gigantic torches hurled headlong in the deep.

He came to see the light change one more time,
Because he needed to behold this earth again,
Needed to touch its edges, feel its familiar form,

Though he it was had emptied out its meaning
He kept coming back to that innocent old thing,
The sweet world he had destroyed so long ago.

Tea Table

Once they said the world lay on a tea table,
And now, that if this universe should rest
In nothingness, still it is of a size,
A shape described by lapsed time, by the speed
Of light, as all that will not reach our eyes
In ages since these explosions have taken place
Remains locked in an absence, cannot be,
So that our limits form an enchanted round
Beyond which nothing anywhere knows of itself.
Dividing good light from the difficult dark,
It is the human, always, measures out the night,
Separating what there is along the edge
Of what we see, and inside that huge horizon
Exists the scent of autumn, its certain sweet decay;
Exist certain gestures made by bodies we have loved;
Exist our myths and the sound of certain words.
Inside are explanations, couched in quaint *argot,*
And outside—(how awful not to be observed
By such passing things as we are!)—outside . . .
The world, it seems, rests on a tea table
Balanced on the backs of enormous elephants
Which stand on the shell of a single tortoise;
And what the tortoise stands on who's to say.

The Lines Between the Stars

Though they seem bent in earnest, seem applications
Of an ordinance, some ultimate authority, seem,
The lines between us and what we see, distinctions
Drawn as fine as our divinings, seem, the paths
Between the immolations, those signal fires built
At the outposts of our ignorance, and the shadows
They trigger on the retinal wall, unwavering,
Seem unswerving as a stone dropped at our feet,
As the bee-line each one of us is making to an end,
Yet the course taken by those portents is crooked,
A circuitous route reflecting more than meets the eye,
A warped trajectory composed of hyperbolic curves,
Of attractive mass and its delicate reciprocation,
So that the light that approaches us around corners
Of gravitation comes careening out of the universe
Like a kid off the roller coaster at Luna Park,
Comes snarled as the skein of memories each of us
Spends a lifetime plucking and rewinding, though
Light seems so sure, so ineluctable, though they seem
So straight and swift, the lines between the stars.

Versicles

If you lift a thing to hold it in your hands—
Any artifact, any burden, any object of your attention, of your joy—
Between your flesh and the flesh of that you hold
Lies a gulf your fingers will never reach across,
An area of slight apparitions that spin and sparkle and crackle
    within themselves,
An unfathomable abyss, the layer of atoms your touch can never
    pierce,
And in that minute chasm the life we know takes place.
Do you think to raise your hand in anger, offended by the crude
    disorder that confronts you every day?
Let your hand fall at your side, for your fist will never find its mark,
    and the stone you throw falls short.
The man that despises, the hating woman, escape your gestures of
    revenge.
And if you long even to the point of tears to extend your hand in
    pity, in adoration?
O, your arm will never find those shoulders and your tenderness
    has no home outside your heart.
Peace my friends, peace you enemies: though the blow falls and the
    guts spill,
Still each of us remains untouched, wrapped in the stuff of
    nothingness,
Appareled in the finest garb, in an airy thinness that glints, that
    glistens,
Each of us cradled till the day we die in swaddling bands of space,
Draped in translucent garments, vested with infinite beauty,
Clad in the underclothes of angels.

The Fairy Tale that Grew Up

In light of the sun setting among gathering clouds,
And considering the countryside had grown gloomy,
With muddy ice collecting in the rutted fields
And stripped trees black as gibbets against the sky,
Considering no steps could be taken that might lead
Back to the verdant memory of your naïve beginning,
The crooked house you happened on wasn't uninviting.
Hard to say at first if it might be inhabited:
No smoke rose from its chimney, though cold bit hard,
And the guttering illumination of its windowpanes
Might have been the last reflections of the day.
But it was candlelight, and the hearth held coals;
Your cries and insistent knock eliciting no answer,
You had forced the flimsy door and walked right in.
A table stood in the obscure room you entered,
And on it lay an open book lit by a single taper.
The house was quiet, and the interior so shadowed,
That though space was small and his chair hard by,
You somehow hadn't seen the stranger till he spoke:
"How old am I?" he asked, and you said he was old,
For his shriveled hands shook, and his beard flowed,
And his faint voice surely had been silent many years.
Dark colors glittered in his robe, and the soft light
Gleamed in the wispy aureole of his white hair.
"Pass me the book," he said, and you did, glancing
At the unknown language there, its cryptic annotation.
He seemed to have no other thought for you, but read,
And in his mouth that indecipherable text became
A glorious history you had heard somewhere before,
Had disremembered and longed for more than you knew,
Of distant origins along the flowered banks of rivers,
Of an inevitable end in loud fire and crevassed earth.
His harshest words seemed strangely sweet, and suddenly
The chamber filled with ghosts, harmonious voices,
Your whole body resonating wildly with that choir.
The sound that issued your ears accepted lovingly,

As you joined that complex canticle and wept for joy;
And then it was gone, and the stranger gone as well.
Those silk sleeves lay disembodied on the floor,
And the old man was dust, an inspiration of the place.
Struck dumb, you stared awhile, searching the empty air;
Then you drew on the robe and drew the book to you.
You sat at last in the old light of an eternal candle,
And in that lambency you thought you finally understood,
Thought each serif of that script had been embellished
Just for you, as you started from the first grand line
And relished every word, attended every implication,
Reading long into the unending night that fell
And waiting for the unknown traveler to arrive.

Of the Knowledge of Good and Evil

Perhaps in the dead of some different night,
Staring into an ocean of as yet unnamed stars
About whose myriad formations we can only surmise;
Perhaps in the heat of a meridional afternoon,
Sprawled beside a water hole in the lush shade
Afforded by primitive plants, lazily swatting flies;
Or perhaps while smeared with grease from the carcass,
Having gorged at long last on a feast of raw flesh,
Listening contentedly to the sounds of digestion—
Into what immense mind on what terrible occasion
Did that thought, that first idea, finally arrive?
Salve homo, I see you there, struck by your sapience,
Stunned by the source of all bitterness and joy,
Conceiving behind wild eyes and a thickset brow
The origin of so much beauty, of so many misdeeds,
Of every identical dread: the origin of the species.
Somewhere great clouds of insects must be swarming,
For you hear their furious humming fill the air;
Somewhere a taloned beast must be tearing its prey,
For you scent the sweet odor of blood on the breeze.
You with the hairy belly, with the heavy jaw ajar,
I see you there, your mind leaping to conclusions:
The cold sweat bursts forth and you twirl a twig,
Idly, abstractedly, envisioning so many things
(Stones piled on each other, bones heaped in a pit),
Imagining every end, getting it all in an instant,
The dissolution of that time and place, of you,
Its mockeries and implication.

Quotidian

Once again we rose as the light fell on our faces
And stumbled out into dust and gathering heat.
At a stream's edge we bent to wash the dreams
Out of our eyes and slake the persistent thirst
That dogged us through the desert of our sleep;
But mere water would not cleanse us of illusions,
Could not assuage the caustic emptiness we felt,
And we wandered off as always, a ragged, lethal band.
Across the table land and among blue hills beyond,
We straggled to and fro, searching out the shade,
Seeking a certain landscape, hunting its ample glade,
For surely it lay waiting as it lay hidden in our hearts.
We did not find it, though, that day nor any other,
The grove, abundant locus, the munificent locale,
And so we made ourselves content with the area at hand,
Scarring it, blooding it, savaging a world
That promised ease and so much satisfaction
And gave us only this.

Great Stone Face

Perhaps something ought to be said about how deadpan
It all is, your experience as it is called, although
It seems you are its, really, rather than vice versa;
How for all your convulsive sobbing, laughter and pity,
It never sheds a tear or tips a wink, never betrays
Even the merest flicker of amusement.
It's hard making your mind up without any hints,
And someone should say something about how you feel
You are never quite getting the point, about how
Every time the bucket plunges deeper down the well
To haul up the subtle something glittering there,
A pause for thought arrives to cancel understanding,
Make nonsense of your efforts at an accurate account.
Of course, it's just such uncertainty that makes us
What we are, just this tremendous reserve in things
That leads us to expect an object of our curiosity
And sets us sifting the air of spring afternoons
In search of whatever it could be that brings
The astonishing crocus to life beneath our feet
And splashes forsythia about in fauvist strokes.
The distance it all keeps is what keeps you looking
(Through language, through landscape's irregular grammar)
For what it is that enthralls you so, what it is
That draws you forth to shiver like the flowering leaves,
And that will someday put you down, an exhausted thing,
Will cast you back upon some inscrutable conclusion,
Letting you drop out of a vast indifference, out
Of some private dissatisfaction, releasing you
One day in an uneasy response all its own.

Nostalgie de la Boue

They took away the changeable sky, all that bad weather,
Took away the sun rising and climbing, shimmering and setting,
And gave him his favorite color always and a constant temperature,
Seventy-one degrees Fahrenheit, adjusted upward in the case of
    wind.
They took away the hate and love that had plagued him so,
The appetites that drew him by the nose, the idea of revenge,
Told him he could grow up now, that such concepts were
    undignified,
Were undeserving of the tremendous thing that was happening now
    on earth.
When the first notes of the overture sounded, the ideal all
    composers had struggled toward,
They instructed him to put those thoughts away, all that
    homesickness and outmoded memory,
All that claptrap and paraphernalia, that obsessive interest in the
    self.
Because it didn't matter anymore what the wailing sounded like,
Now that the ragweed was resurrected and the positrons were back
    in place;
Now that all energies were evenly distributed
Nobody cared any longer about the future or what light might look
    like on the stone;
No one wished to hear the bedtime stories told again,
Now that the final, ecstatic, inhuman celebration had begun.
But there, amidst that indistinguishable blaze,
He missed his own blue sky, its wild suggestion,
Missed the iciest rainfall sweeping from the clouds,
And missed his heartache, too, his hope deferred;
As the triumph of so much perfection was announced,
He wished even for the dark ferries moving slowly through the
    dawn,
Wanted back those flowered barges gliding silently to nowhere,
Oh, he longed for those black boats most of all.

As the Romans Do

When you've had your morning coffee on the street
With a fierce political journal and brandy on the side,
When you've waved to Gianni, Pippo, Mauro and Maria,
When you've chatted with Nina, said how good she looks,
When you've described for Antonio in no uncertain terms
The sort of retribution your football team deserves,
When you've yawned, stretched, thoroughly digested
And walked the winding alleyway to the public square,
Then, as the sun appears suddenly above the roofline
Of churches and cafés, and the blue-white sky descends
Right down to the pavement and to you, the light it bears
Scattering over the ornate fountain you stand beside,
So that a coruscating reflection of blaze and shade
Forms an intricate design more fascinating than fire,
A warp and weft of constant motion, no more to be grasped
Than the flickering chiaroscuro of your own thoughts . . .
Then, reaching out to steady yourself on the incised stone,
Raise a hand in mute salutation, to the shifting pattern
That passes before you, to a future forever about to happen
Here in this ancient place crowded with the past,
Where the waters leap upward like a voice within you
And the sunlight comes down to gild your turbulence,
In Rome, in Rome, *paisano,* do as they all must do.

Loihi

for T.N. Danforth

Three thousand feet beneath a tranquil sea,
A hot spot troubles the Pacific floor,
As lava thrust from earth's convulsive core
Has formed a crater where an isle will be.

That hidden world was lavishly displayed
To divers in a research submarine,
Who drifted on a landscape unforeseen:
Bacteria, in layers like red brocade,

Draped basalt pinnacles and overhangs,
Shimmering in a dense volcanic gas
That took the unaccustomed light like glass.

A monster of the deep, all jaws and fangs,
Lives there; it dies if brought up to our day,
Where waves are now, and palms will someday sway.

The Year of the Comet

Appearing "like a blowtorch in the sky,"
It lit the night, and thus the naked eye
At that time had no trouble in discerning
What seemed for all the world to be a burning
Bit of heaven, a rending of the veil
Of the firmament, though in fact the tail,
Composed of meteoric dust and gas,
Held little to combust, so that it was
Merely one more reflection of sunlight
Arriving out of darkness to ignite
Quick imaginations of idle men,
Seventy-six years past, in 1910.
For some, the comet heralded an age
Of science, in which mankind would engage
Ultimate questions and prevail, in which
Technical advances would enrich
Our lives and a benighted populace,
As seeing means belief, rise to embrace
The light of reason lately come in view;
For others, as belief is seeing, too,
The visitation meant apocalypse,
Wherein the comet's orbital ellipse
Had brought it back on an appointed round
To signal that the earth would soon be drowned
In blood, the seals be broken, the sky catch
Fire, that helpless sinners would soon watch
A hapless world destroyed and kingdom come,
For if the biblical millenium
Was winding down, then judgment day was due.
Well, we were ripe for change, that much was true,
And both persuasions, in a sense, have been
Vindicated, as modern medicine
Works new miracles to extend our years,
While modern warfare brings this vale of seers
To the point of prophecies that have gone
Beyond the wildest visions of St. John;

Yet aren't they both evasions of the present,
Utopia and doom, predictions pleasant
Or otherwise, but easy answers to
The daily mix-ups we must muddle through?
So men still mire in misery every day,
While earth still spins along its merry way,
Through days of bliss and seasons of distress
And eons of redundant emptiness.
The brightest memories occasioned by
Such hours pass in the twinkling of an I,
And once again the average life transpires
Amidst the sort of era that acquires
Historians but leaves the bard non-plussed,
Three quarters of a century that must
Like every other in its time, appear
To its inhabitants as the nadir
Of human kindness and the height of sense;
Meanwhile, a "dirty snowball" circumvents
An end in space, accelerating through
Our solar system toward its rendezvous
With sunshine, with the spectacles of men,
And Halley's comet has come back again.
I went out to look for it late last night;
You would have laughed to see me, for in light
Of nearby towns and in my ignorance
Of stars, I didn't stand a snowball's chance
In Dante's hottest hell, where lost souls sigh
Because they cannot see the nighttime sky.
Oh, I may have seen something, I suppose,
An unimpressive squib of light that rose
In the southwest with Pegasus and might,
If it wasn't a plane, or satellite,
Or weather balloon, or simply a spot
On my binoculars, as like as not
Have been a comet; that's the tale I plan
To tell the children as an aged man,
At any rate, how once, blazoned above
Me, I beheld the very sign that wove
Its way into the Bayeaux tapestry
When, waiting on the tide of history,
Norman troops stood by the channel, how I

Witnessed the same sight seen by the Magi,
As Giotto pictured them in 1301,
Making their augured journey to the Son,
How light observed in Aristotle's time,
And subsequently hailed as the sublime
In the Philosopher's philosophy,
Has showered down its countenance on me,
Who have, I think, as much a right as these
To light streaming like "long hair in the breeze,"
As the phrase goes whence "comet" is derived.
But truth to tell, what notions had survived
In me to the grave age of thirty-three
Of some grand cosmic continuity
Stretching across generations of men
And offering a type of order when
Life here on earth is at its most confused
Died in thirty seconds, and disabused
Of superstition, I went back inside
To soothe chagrin with thoughts that I had tried
To see it, that the world had grown too old
For auguries, and that my toes were cold.
Indoors, warming myself in the bright glow
And cold comfort cast by a picture show,
I switched the channel to the late-night news,
Where, among speeches, sports and interviews,
The audience was treated to the sight
Of footage filmed aboard a plane in flight,
Featuring what resembled a small comma
In space that punctuated the ring drama
Of its recurrence with a mild display
Of radiance enhanced by cathode ray;
And so I saw the object after all,
If not first hand, then in a crystal ball,
The second sight of this dim century,
That dispiriting medium, TV.
I watched awhile and then shut off the set,
Stood up, let in the dog, and went to get
A drink before I let the cat out, locked
The house up and turned in; the ice-cubes rocked
In my glass, clucking sympathy, while framed
Within a windowpane, tiny stars flamed

Enormously in the immense inane;
It seemed whatever musings might explain
The disconcerting music of those spheres
Had ceased to matter much, as no one hears
Anything like harmony in the skies
And comets are snuffed out before our eyes.
Somewhere that misplaced punctuation mark
Awaited faint distinctions in the dark,
But I had vigils of my own to keep
And made my way upstairs and so to sleep,
Leaving the melting remnants of my drink
To come to nothing at the kitchen sink
And wishing other viewers more success
When next the comet comes from emptiness
(If it does come, if our poor atmosphere
Is not pure smog, if we are even here)
To set its blazing match-head to the straw
Of human intellect and then withdraw,
Wheeling around its perihelion
And disappearing with the tail it spun.

A Note About the Author

George Bradley was born in Roslyn, New York, and graduated from Yale University in 1975. His first book of poems, *Terms to Be Met,* was chosen by James Merrill as the winning volume in the 1985 Yale Series of Younger Poets competition. In 1990 he was chosen by Mona Van Duyn to receive the Peter I. B. Lavan Younger Poets Award from the Academy of American Poets. He lives in Chester, Connecticut.

A Note on the Type

This book is set in a typeface called Méridien, a classic roman designed by Adrian Frutiger for the French type foundry Deberny et Peignot in 1957. Adrian Frutiger was born in Interlaken, Switzerland, in 1928 and studied type design there and at the Kunstgewerbeschule in Zurich. In 1953 he moved to Paris, where he joined Deberny et Peignot as a member of the design staff. Méridien, as well as his other typeface of world renown, Univers, was created for the Lumitype photo-set machine.

Composition by Graphic Composition, Inc.,
Athens, Georgia
Printed and bound by Halliday Lithographers,
West Hanover, Massachusetts